Saltwater Fishing

By Laura Purdie Salas

Consultant:
Forbes Darby
Special Projects Director
American Sportfishing Association
Alexandria, Virginia

Capstone
press

Mankato, Minnesota

Capstone High-Interest Books are published by Capstone Press
151 Good Counsel Drive, P.O. Box 669, Mankato, Minnesota 56002
www.capstonepress.com

Salas, Laura Purdie.
    Saltwater fishing/by Laura Purdie Salas.
    p. cm.—(The great outdoors)
    ISBN 0-7368-2412-X
    1. Saltwater fishing—Juvenile literature. [1. Saltwater fishing. 2. Fishing.]
I. Title. II. Series.
SH457.S27 2004
799.16—dc22   2003018353

Summary: Describes the equipment, skills, conservation issues, and safety
    concerns of saltwater fishing.

Editorial Credits

James Anderson, editor; Timothy Halldin, series designer; Molly Nei,
    book designer and illustrator; Jo Miller, photo researcher

Photo Credits

Ann and Rob Simpson, 15
Capstone Press/Gary Sundermeyer, cover (bottom right), 9, 21
Comstock, 1 (background)
Corbis/Bill Schild, cover (top); Dale C. Spartas, 12, 33; Dan Lamont, 16;
    Joel W. Sheagren, 19; Joseph Sohm/ChromoSohm, Inc., 30; Mugshots, 26; Neil
    Rabinowitz, 4; Reuters NewMedia Inc., 36; Sygma, 35; Tom Stewart, 7; Tony
    Arruza, 29
Creatas, 21 (background)
Getty Images/JPR, 10
photo courtesy of the Alaska Sealife Center, 42 (top)
Seapics.com/Doug Perrine, 40 (top); Doug Stamm, 22, 42 (bottom), 43; Masa
    Uishoda 39, 40 (bottom), 41 (bottom); Richard Herrmann, 41 (top); Walt Stearns,
    cover (bottom left), 25

1 2 3 4 5 6 09 08 07 06 05 04

Table of Contents

FORTUNE

SAN DIEGO, CA.

4

CHAPTER 1

Saltwater Fishing

Saltwater fishing is a popular activity around the world. People who saltwater fish are called anglers. North American anglers fish in the Atlantic and Pacific Oceans or the Gulf of Mexico. They fish from boats, piers, and the shore.

People have been catching fish for thousands of years. Anglers once tied a line around a sharp piece of bone, wood, or shell. They put the sharp piece inside bait, such as a small fish. The anglers pulled the line tight when a larger fish swallowed the bait. The sharp piece caught in the fish's mouth.

Saltwater fishing is a popular sport.

The United States' first president was a saltwater angler. In 1790, newspaper reporters wrote about President George Washington's fishing trips. Washington fished for sea bass and blackfish.

Many recent presidents have fished. President George H. W. Bush fished near his family's land in Maine. He fished for bluefish for 18 days in 1989.

Bodyguards crowded around him in their own boats and may have scared the fish away. Bush fished for 17 days without a bite. He finally caught a 10-pound (4.5-kilogram) bluefish on the last day of his vacation.

Saltwater Fishing Today

People who fish for fun are called recreational anglers. More than 15 million people saltwater fish for fun in the United States. In 2002, these anglers caught about 440 million fish. About 380,000 anglers fish in waters off Canada. They catch more than 7 million fish each year.

Commercial fishers catch fish to sell.

Saltwater fishing is an important industry in North America. People who sell their catch for money are called commercial fishers. They sell fish to supermarkets and restaurants. Commercial fishers caught almost 100 times as many fish as recreational anglers in 2002.

North American anglers have plenty of coastline from which to fish. The United States has more than 90,000 miles (145,000 kilometers) of coastline. Canada has more than 149,000 miles (240,000 kilometers) of coastline.

Modern equipment helps make saltwater fishing easy for many people. Stronger rods and lines allow anglers to catch bigger fish. Depth finders help anglers locate areas where fish may be. Faster boats let anglers cover large areas.

Types of Fish

Anglers around the world try to catch more than 700 types of saltwater fish. Many people fish in the oceans for sport fish. A few types of sport fish are marlin, sailfish, and sharks. These fish are not caught for food but for the thrill and challenge of the catch.

Most fish caught in salt water can be eaten. Some anglers focus on catching fish like halibut, cod, and tuna.

Tuna Teriyaki

Ingredients:
4 tuna steaks
⅓ cup (80 mL) soy sauce
1 tablespoon (15 mL) honey
1 tablespoon (15 mL) chopped ginger
1 teaspoon (5 mL) minced garlic
2 tablespoons (30 mL) vegetable oil

Equipment:
9-inch by 13-inch (23-centimeter
    by 33-centimeter) glass
    baking dish
cooking spray
medium bowl
metal spatula
mixing spoon
pastry brush

What You Do:
1. Lightly coat baking dish with cooking spray.
2. Place steaks in baking dish.
3. In bowl, make marinade by mixing soy sauce, honey, ginger, garlic, and vegetable oil.
4. Pour the marinade over the tuna steaks.
5. Place in refrigerator to marinate for 30 minutes.
6. Use pastry brush to brush tops of steaks with marinade.
7. Broil or grill for 4 minutes, about 4 to 6 inches (10 to 15 centimeters) from heat source.
8. Turn steaks over with metal spatula. Brush marinade over steaks.
9. Broil or grill for 4 more minutes.

Serves: 4   *Children should have adult supervision.*

Equipment

Saltwater anglers use many items to catch fish. Basic equipment includes rods and reels, line, and bait. Serious anglers may use other equipment such as boats, electronic items, and a variety of tools.

Rods and Reels

Saltwater anglers use fishing rods made from graphite or fiberglass. These rods bend easily. Saltwater fishing rods are between 5 and 12 feet (2 and 4 meters) long.

Rods have a reel attached to them. Reels hold the fishing line. Reels allow anglers to cast and collect the line. Anglers turn a crank on the reel to pull in the line.

Most saltwater fishing equipment is larger than gear used for freshwater fishing.

Lines

Fishing line attaches to the hook. It allows anglers to pull in the catch. Anglers use line that is strong enough for the fish they are trying to catch. Any fishing line can be broken. A strong fish can break a line if an angler is not paying attention.

Anglers use the line to make the fish tired. Fish are strong and can break the line. Anglers must keep and release tension on the line to avoid breaking the line. Anglers must keep a good hold on the line to keep the fish hooked. But too much tension can break the line.

Bringing in a Fish

The angler must make a decision once the fish is close to the boat. Some anglers do not want to keep the fish they catch. They might release the fish without lifting it into the boat.

Anglers use gaffs, leaders, or nets to bring the fish into the boat. A gaff is a large metal hook with a handle. Anglers stick their catch with the hook. They use the handle to help pull up the fish.

An angler uses a gaff to lift a large tarpon into the boat.

A leader is a piece of strong wire that attaches the fishing line to the hook. It is much stronger than fishing line. A leader can handle the weight of heavy fish.

Bait and Lures

Saltwater anglers use many types of live bait. Small fish are the most popular bait. The size of the bait depends on the size of the fish an angler is trying to catch. An angler might use a 2-pound (1-kilogram) mullet to catch a 15-pound (7-kilogram) tuna. Large chunks of tuna might be used to catch a 500-pound (227-kilogram) tiger shark. Live bait includes shrimp, crabs, worms, and shellfish.

Anglers use natural bait to make chum. Anglers place cut-up fish in a net bag and drag it behind the boat. The blood and oil from the fish create a smelly trail in the water for other fish to follow. Fish that follow chum are easier to catch. Mackerel, snapper, and tuna are a few fish that anglers attract with chum.

Lures are brightly colored to look like a fish's natural food.

Anglers also use lures. These artificial objects attract fish. Lures are made of feathers, metal, plastic, wood, yarn, and other materials.

Some lures look like a fish's natural food. Flies are lures that look like insects. People make flies from feathers or animal hair. Imitations are plastic lures that look like frogs, earthworms, and small fish. Plugs are wooden lures that look like small fish.

Anglers take cruisers on long fishing trips.

Boats

Anglers use many kinds of fishing boats. Some anglers use small utility boats. Utility boats are 12 to 18 feet (4 to 5 meters) long. These boats are usually made of wood, aluminum, or fiberglass. Utility boats are best for calm water.

Anglers who travel on rough water use cruisers. These boats range from 18 to 40 feet (5 to 12 meters) long. Cruisers travel faster than utility boats. They have a cabin. They often have areas below the deck called berths. People can sit or lie down in berths. Anglers can make overnight trips on cruisers with sleeping space in the berths.

Some anglers rent a spot on a party boat. Party boats depart on a regular schedule and often stay out all day. A spot on a party boat can cost from $30 to more than $100. Some party boats have tackle for anglers to use or rent. Most anglers bring their own tackle. Some party boats hold more than 100 anglers.

One angler or a small group of anglers can rent a charter boat for fishing. A guide from the charter company runs the boat. The guide also gives advice about fishing. A charter boat usually costs $300 or more per person to rent for a day.

Some saltwater anglers do not use a boat. They fish from shore. Fishing from the shore is called surf fishing. Other anglers fish from piers and bridges.

Clothing

Anglers protect themselves from sun, wind, and water. Hats protect their face and head from sunburn. Sunglasses reduce the glare of the sun on the water.

Waterproof jackets and pants keep anglers dry and warm. Waterproof boots or shoes are helpful because the bottom of the boat often gets wet. Surf fishers who wade into water also need waterproof boots.

Most anglers wear jackets and vests with lots of pockets. Anglers store lures and other items in the pockets. Jackets and shirts must be loose around the shoulders and arms. Loose-fitting clothing allows the angler to cast easily.

Other Items

Anglers carry other gear. They use sinkers and bobbers. Sinkers are small metal weights that hold the bait deeper in the water. Bobbers float on the surface and keep the bait from sinking too far.

Proper clothing keeps an angler warm and dry.

Anglers carry tools. They use pliers to repair tackle. They also carry tools to remove hooks from fish, clean their catch, and weigh their catch.

Some anglers use electronic equipment. Depth finders use sound waves to find objects underwater. Depth finders have a screen where anglers can see images of the ocean floor.

Anglers may carry contour maps of the area where they are fishing. These maps show the formation of the ocean's floor. Certain formations in the ground tell anglers how deep the water is. Anglers then match the length of their line with the depth of the water.

Most saltwater anglers are skilled with nautical charts and use them to navigate. These charts show the coastline and the depth of the water. They also show tides, lighthouses, and other items to help anglers find their way on the ocean.

A global positioning system (GPS) allows anglers to find their favorite fishing spots and to navigate safely. A GPS uses satellites in space to find a location. A GPS can also help anglers who are lost in a storm.

jacket

lure

sunglasses

PFD

bait pail

fishing pole

fishing line

hat

depth finder

filet knife

net

pliers

Equipment

- bait pail
- depth finder
- filet knife
- fishing line
- fishing pole
- hat
- jacket
- lures
- net
- PFD (personal flotation device)
- pliers
- sunglasses

21

CHAPTER 3

Skills and Techniques

Saltwater anglers build up knowledge and experience to make good decisions. They learn about the best places to fish. They find out what time of day that fish are most active. They also must know how to choose bait and fishing methods.

Locations

Knowing about fish habitats can help anglers decide where to fish. Fish prefer certain areas to feed and swim. Anglers need to know the usual location of the fish they want to catch.

An angler chooses the right bait and location to catch a barracuda.

Some fish like to feed near strong currents. Large fish eat small fish and shrimp that the currents carry. Many anglers like to fish when the tide is coming in or going out. When the tide shifts, fish look for food in the currents.

Some fish like to swim in warm water. These fish include sailfish, marlin, and tiger sharks. Shallow water is often warmer than deep water.

Other types of fish live in colder water. Cod and Atlantic mackerel are two species that live in cold water.

Most fish need good cover. Fish hide in cover underwater. Cover might be a wrecked ship, coral reefs, or the space between the posts that hold up a pier. Groupers and snapper are two fish species that often swim near coral reefs.

When to Fish

Saltwater anglers choose their fishing time based on what kind of fish they want to catch. Fish are more active during feeding

Anglers catch sailfish in warm water.

periods. Snook feed day and night, but sharks feed more at night. Anglers learn the active times for different fish species.

Anglers also choose their fishing time based on their fishing spot. Nighttime is best for pier fishing. Bait fish are attracted to the lights around the pier. Anglers catch the bigger fish that come to feed on the bait fish.

Fishing Methods

There are many ways to saltwater fish. Some common methods are surf fishing, drift fishing, still fishing, trolling, and jigging.

Surf fishers usually catch the most fish in the early morning or late evening. During the daytime, sandy beaches offer no cover. During the early morning and late evening, the sun casts more shadows. Fish use shadowy water as cover.

To drift fish, an angler lets the boat drift in the current. An angler can use the still fish method from a pier or an anchored boat. The angler lets the bait stay in the water. Still and drift fishers might catch giant sea bass, rockfish, and barracuda.

An angler uses a moving boat to troll. The angler lets the line trail behind the boat. An angler can troll while walking on a bridge

Surf fishers do much of their fishing during early morning and late evening hours.

or pier. They let the line trail as they walk. Trolling is a good way to catch groupers, bluefish, tuna, and marlin.

Anglers in an anchored boat or on a pier or bridge can also jig. Anglers who jig let the lure fall down and then jerk it up again. They keep the lure moving constantly.

Fish that are attracted to movement might strike a jig. These fish include grunts, black sea bass, and some kinds of tuna. The fish may leap out of the water when they go after a jigging lure.

While trolling, anglers let their line fall behind a moving boat.

29

DANGER
BEACH
CLOSE

CHAPTER 4

Conservation

Responsible anglers protect fish and their habitats. The sport of saltwater fishing depends on clean water and healthy fish.

Licenses and Regulations

Government groups set rules for anglers. Anglers may need to buy a license in order to fish. License sales tell the government how many people go fishing and where they like to fish.

Laws set limits on the number of fish an angler can take home each day. Different types of fish have different limits. Limits make sure that there will be fish left for other anglers.

Government groups also decide minimum sizes of fish that can be caught. Anglers must release fish that are too small. These rules help fish survive long enough to reproduce.

Polluted beaches must be cleaned before anglers can fish from the water.

Releasing Fish

Anglers release fish they do not want to keep. They put the fish back into the water. They also release fish that are not legal to keep. This form of fishing is called catch-and-release.

Anglers handle fish gently to avoid injuring the fish. Anglers try to remove the hook while the fish is in water. A fish out of water cannot breathe. A fish will die if it spends too much time out of the water.

Protecting Water Sources

Responsible anglers keep water clean. Polluted water enters fish's bodies and can make fish sick. It can even kill fish. Waste from farming, industry, and cars can pollute the ocean.

Anglers can help conservation efforts by acting responsibly. They should leave the ocean as clean as or cleaner than they found it. They should not throw litter into the ocean.

An angler releases a bonefish he does not want to keep.

Oil Spills

Oil spills are a major water pollutant. Large ships carrying oil have crashed and spilled oil into the oceans. The oil has damaged fish habitats. Many sea animals such as birds, sea otters, and whales have also been destroyed by oil spills.

The *Exxon Valdez* caused the largest oil spill in recent history. The tanker became stuck on the Bligh Reef off the coast of Alaska. The ship crashed on March 24, 1989. The ship spilled 11 million gallons (42 million liters) of oil into the Pacific Ocean.

The oil killed millions of fish and other animals. The total cost of cleaning the spill was more than $2 billion. The fishing industry was hurt by the spill. Many fishing companies had to find other places to fish.

People work together to clean beaches and water after an oil spill.

36

CHAPTER 5

Safety

Saltwater fishing can be dangerous. Bad weather can threaten fishing boats on the ocean. Anglers should always wear PFDs while in the boat. They should know the weather reports. Anglers should always fish with a partner, and they should have rescue skills.

Weather

Anglers check the weather forecast before leaving shore. They stay on land if storms are predicted. They also check wave height. Many anglers do not go on the water if waves are taller than 3 feet (1 meter).

Anglers watch for lightning in the sky. Lightning often strikes the highest target. Anglers take down fishing rods and stay as low in the boat as possible. They move to shore when they see lightning.

Hurricanes and other storms can cause great damage to boats.

Dressing Safely

Storms are not the only weather dangers. Anglers need to protect themselves from sunburn. They wear sunscreen on any uncovered skin. They also wear hats and sunglasses.

Anglers need warm, dry clothes. Anglers usually have an extra set of dry clothes. They should wear a waterproof outer layer of clothing. Anglers should be prepared for changing weather conditions.

Equipment Safety

Saltwater anglers handle dangerous objects. Fish hooks, knives, and gaffs should always be placed where people will not cut themselves.

Safety is a big concern for many anglers. Following safety rules is important. Safe anglers make saltwater fishing an enjoyable sport for everyone.

Anglers use hats or visors and sunglasses to protect them from the sun's rays.

Bluefish

Description: Bluefish are blue along the top and silver on the sides. They have two dorsal fins. Bluefish have sharp teeth. They usually weigh 3 to 15 pounds (1 to 7 kilograms).
Habitat: near the surface, around coastal areas and structures
Food: smaller fish
Bait and lures: menhaden, herring, chum, flies, jigs

Black Grouper

Description: Black groupers have olive or gray bodies with black spots. They usually weigh around 10 pounds (5 kilograms). Groupers are powerful for their size.
Habitat: offshore reefs, shipwrecks, ridges, ocean bottom
Food: smaller fish
Bait and lures: pinfish, grunts, goggleyes, leadhead jigs

40

Bluefin Tuna

Description: The bluefin tuna's blue color fades to silver on its side and belly. These slim fish can grow to almost 1,500 pounds (680 kilograms).
Habitat: deep water, but they come close to the surface to feed
Food: mackerel, herring, squid, bluefish
Bait and lures: mackerel, skipjack, spoons, jigs, plastic squid

Blue Marlin

Description: Blue marlin are bright blue on top, fading to silver on the sides and belly. Some grow as heavy as 1,500 pounds (680 kilograms).
Habitat: deep waters, warm offshore water, weedy areas
Food: bonito, tuna, dolphin
Bait and lures: trolling with mackerel, bonito, lures that dive and bubble

Pacific Halibut

Description: Pacific halibut are dark on one side. Both eyes are on this side. Its other side is light. Halibut swim with the light side facing the ocean floor. Some pacific halibut can grow as large as 450 pounds (204 kilograms).

Habitat: deep, cold water; areas with flat bottoms of mud, sand, or gravel; areas with strong currents

Food: herring, smaller fish

Bait and lures: herring with heavy tackle, heavy jigs, sinking flies

Striped Bass

Description: Striped bass are called stripers. Stripers are silver. They have 7 or 8 stripes along each side. They usually weigh 5 to 10 pounds (2 to 5 kilograms). They can grow as large as 75 pounds (34 kilograms).

Habitat: in bays and close to shore in both salt and freshwater

Food: herring

Bait and lures: squid, herring, crabs, jigs, flies

Glossary

aluminum (uh-LOO-mi-nuhm)—a lightweight metal; utility boats are sometimes made of aluminum.

artificial (ar-ti-FISH-uhl)—made by people

berth (BURTH)—a bed in a boat

conservation (kon-sur-VAY-shuhn)—the protection of things, such as ocean water and animals

dorsal fins (DORE-sel FINS)—fins that appear on the backs of fish

fiberglass (FYE-bur-glass)—a strong material made from fine threads of glass

graphite (GRAF-ite)—a lightweight material used to make fishing poles

habitat (HAB-uh-tat)—the natural place where animals live

nautical (NAW-tuh-kuhl)—to do with ships, sailing, or navigation

Read More

Hopkins, Ellen. *Freshwater Fishing.* The Great Outdoors. Mankato, Minn.: Capstone Press, 2002.

Salas, Laura Purdie. *Ice Fishing.* The Great Outdoors. Mankato, Minn.: Capstone Press, 2002.

Travis, George. *Let's Go Fishing in the Ocean.* Let's Go Fishing. Vero Beach, Fla.: Rourke, 1998.

You can also read about saltwater fishing in magazines such as *Sport Fishing* and *Saltwater Fly Fishing.*

Useful Addresses

American Sportfishing Association
225 Reinekers Lane
Suite 420
Alexandria, VA 22314

Canadian Wildlife Service
Environment Canada
Ottawa, ON K1A 0H3
Canada

U.S. Fish and Wildlife Service
Fish and Wildlife Reference Service
5430 Grosvenor Lane
Suite 110
Bethesda, MD 20814

Internet Sites

FactHound offers a safe, fun way to find Internet sites related to this book. All of the sites on FactHound have been researched by our staff.

Here's how:
1. Visit *www.facthound.com*
2. Type in this special code **073682412X** for age-appropriate sites. Or enter a search word related to this book for a more general search.
3. Click on the **Fetch It** button.

FactHound will fetch the best sites for you!

Index